T0009897

A

SMALL BOOK
OF
EXEMPLARY
DEATHS

A

SMALL BOOK

OF

EXEMPLARY

DEATHS

MATT STURROCK

SUTHERLAND HOUSE

TORONTO, 2022

Sutherland House
416 Moore Ave., Suite 205
Toronto, ON M4G 1C9

Copyright © 2022 by Matt Sturrock

All rights reserved, including the right to reproduce this book or
portions thereof in any form whatsoever. For information on rights and
permissions or to request a special discount for bulk purchases, please
contact Sutherland House at info@sutherlandhousebooks.com
Sutherland House and logo are registered trademarks of
The Sutherland House Inc.

First edition, October 2022

If you are interested in inviting one of our authors to a live event or
media appearance, please contact sranasinghe@sutherlandhousebooks.com
and visit our website at sutherlandhousebooks.com for more
information about our authors and their schedules.

Manufactured in China
Cover designed by Lena Yang
Book composed by Karl Hunt
Illustrations by Lara Galustian

Library and Archives Canada Cataloguing in Publication
Title: A small book of exemplary deaths / Matt Sturrock.
Names: Sturrock, Matt, author.
Identifiers: Canadiana 20220210780 |
ISBN 9781989555781 (softcover)
Subjects: LCSH: Death—Miscellanea. |
LCSH: Death—Causes—Miscellanea.
Classification: LCC HQ1073 .S78 2022 |
DDC 306.9—dc23

ISBN 9781989555781

FOREWORD

The genesis of this little book can be traced back to two pieces of writing I came across some years ago. The first was an Englishman's account of the revolutionary Terror unfolding in Paris; in the witness's telling, some of the youthful dandies made to proffer themselves to the guillotine first danced a few steps for the jeering crowd before placing their necks on the block. The second was Clive James's poem on the death of Egon Friedell, the historian, critic, cabaret performer, and Jew who leapt from an upper-story window of his home in Vienna when Nazi brownshirts came to arrest him, and shouted a warning to passers-by on the pavement below so they wouldn't be harmed by his fatal impact. I thought that such a blend of composure and insouciance in the first instance, and such scrupulous decency in the second, were commendable in the extreme; so I started to seek out and collect other examples of that sort of behaviour. I wanted to extol people who demonstrated remarkable physical courage, élan, unflappability, or dignity just before they died. The result was a sort of literary *stele*–the commemoration of an infinitesimally small sample of paragons drawn from an almost illimitable historical supply.

Some may think it needlessly morbid to dwell on such matters, but given that all of us will one day face personal extinction, it seems prudent to learn how to bear such an inevitability through the brave example of others. Michel de Montaigne suggested in his *Essays* that the manner in which a person met his or her end could "give a good or ill repute to their whole life"; for his own part, he hoped to die "handsomely, that is, patiently and without noise". But Montaigne drew heavily from the works of Cicero, who pondered these things nearly 1700 years earlier–and who died well, baring his neck to the hired assassins when they came for him, and calmly urging them to do their duty. Living and dying well are ultimately inextricable. Those who think seriously about the former cannot help but contend with the latter, and such preoccupations seem timeless.

Readers may be surprised not to find more soldiers here, a choice I made partly because the subjects seemed more meritorious if they had not been trained and paid to face death. Instead, one will find a wildly eclectic assortment of men and women: an Alexandrian mathematician, a Haitian slave, a Vietnamese monk, and on it goes. Many of these people lived and died continents and millennia apart. They subscribed to creeds the others in these pages would have found alien and unfathomable. They are thrust together here because of their extraordinary strength of character in the face of annihilation.

In our own day, it's sometimes easy to suppose that these aforementioned virtues are on the wane—that most bystanders at an unfolding tragedy, for instance, would rather record and digitally upload the occasion for the titillation of their social media subscribers than court danger by assisting those in distress. Indeed, it seems that the ignominious fate of uncountable people now living is to merely gawp at a screen for threescore-and-ten years, and to distractedly conduct their meagre affairs in the real world while their minds yearn for the pleasures of the virtual. But maybe we're not quite there yet. Astonishing acts of altruism and bravery are happening all over the world as I write this, and the book, arranged chronologically, records events all the way up to the near-present.

What was necessarily harder than knowing when to stop was when to begin. Too many ancient annals are obscured by fantastical and religiose elements, or are merely the dour financial reckonings of empire. Compelling and well-documented dramas featuring mortals untouched by the divine are quite a recent phenomenon where record-keeping is concerned, and it's only about 2500 years ago, with the Greek city states nearing their cultural zenith, that I found a logical starting point. It seemed impossible not to include the Spartans in this assemblage. Perhaps no other society has so rigorously inculcated the importance of courage in its citizens, and the battle of Thermopylae, that most testing crucible, bristles with worthy subjects who could have been praised here. But the heroes of that encounter, King Leonidas and his outnumbered force, were almost too untroubled and steadfast as they faced their gruesome end. Their zealous comportment can make them strange and remote to the 21st-century reader. And so, I open by counterbalancing the most esteemed Spartiate of the hour (one whose exploits have become the hackneyed stuff of pop culture) with one of his comrades, an altogether more compromised and conflicted figure seeking redemption, before continuing the tortuous march to modernity.

THIS IS FOR:

DIENEKES (D. 480 BCE) . . .

. . . the Spartan citizen-soldier (and perhaps the quickest wit at Western Civilization's most celebrated last stand) who, having been told that the myriad arrows of the enemy would blot out the sun, replied, in unimprovably laconic fashion, "So much the better, we shall fight in the shade."

FOR:

ARISTODEMUS (D. 479 BCE) . . .

. . . Dienekes' peer, who, having been invalided out of action at Thermopylae with an eye infection, and sent back home to Sparta where his unlucky survival was abominated, later fought with such audacious and suicidal valour against the foreign horde on the field at Plataea, that Herodotus, Father of History, adjudged him bravest of all the Greeks that day.

FOR:

SOCRATES (D. 399 BCE) . . .

. . . pug-faced stonemason, ironist, and ethicist who, convicted of impiety and an excess of inconvenient cleverness by the leaders of Athens, honoured his death sentence by drinking hemlock and, while waiting to be overtaken by its lethal effects, cheerfully admonished the inconsolable friends and disciples at his bedside for their histrionics.

FOR:

THE THEBAN COMMANDER,
THEAGENES (D. 338 BCE) . . .

. . . and his elite fighting unit, the 300 paired male lovers comprising the Sacred Band, whose beauty and noble refusal to capitulate at the Battle of Chaeronea so stunned the victor, King Philip of Macedon, that he later wept for their loss as he gazed upon the heap of their cleaved and smashed bodies.

FOR:

SOPHONISBA (D. 203 BCE) . . .

. . . Carthaginian noblewoman and prized prisoner of Scipio Africanus at the close of the Second Punic War, who, without remonstration or qualm, drank from a cup of poison rather than adorn the vast procession of spoils, slaves, and seized exotica that were later flaunted in the triumphal parade in victorious Rome.

THIS IS FOR:

THE LEGATE MARCUS PETREIUS, AND HIS ALLY, KING JUBA OF NUMIDIA (D. 46 BCE) . . .

. . . who, having seen their Republican legions routed at Thapsus in one of the final battles of the Roman Civil War, agreed, with grim courtesy and undaunted mien, to fight a duel to the death rather than surrender to Julius Caesar's approaching minions.

FOR:

THE FORMER SLAVE EPICHARIS
(D. 65 CE) . . .

. . . who, caught on the edges of a plot to remove the cruel, ineffectual, and vainglorious Emperor Nero from power, would not yield the names of her fellow conspirators while being scourged and rent upon the rack, and in a final reproof to her torturers and the miscreant who commanded them, fashioned a noose from her own clothing and exercised the ultimate freedom.

FOR:

IIUA TUO (D. 208) . . .

. . . scholar, herbalist, acupuncturist, and surgeon during the parlous end-stage of China's Han dynasty who, having declined to treat the despotic warlord, Cao Cao, for enfeebling headaches, was arrested, and while awaiting his demise in a cell, wrote and gifted to the jailer a medical treatise of such magisterial detail it might have palliated or saved the lives of unreckonable generations.

FOR:

HYPATIA OF ALEXANDRIA
(D. 415) . . .

. . . astronomer and mathematician, who would not cease her scientific teachings that so threatened the jealous monotheists guarding their own Revelation, and, wisely attuned to life's transience, did not resist or plead as the Patriarch's enforcers set upon her, stabbing and flaying–accidentally making a martyr of a pagan.

FOR:

ADURGUNDBAD (D. 541) . . .

. . . *kanarang* of the Sassanid empire's north-eastern province, who, having been ordered by Khosrow I, King of Kings, to murder a child claimant to the throne, instead chose to hide the boy and raise him in secret, living for ten years under the shadow of discovery, until at last Khosrow's long arm reached out and expunged him for his righteous perfidy.

THIS IS FOR:

DIHYA 'AL-KAHINA' (D. 703) . . .

. . . Berber warrior-queen (despised as a seer and sorceress by her adversaries) who led the last vestiges of resistance against the expanding Umayyad Caliphate in North Africa, until, prophesying her own end, she entrusted the care and future of her two sons to one of her own Arab hostages, and rode out into the desert to join battle a final time.

FOR:

OLAF TRYGVASSON (D. 1000) . . .

. . . a raider and usurper who, ambushed off the coast of Wendland by a party of men just as violent as he, laughingly insulted his assailants as they grappled onto the deck of his longship and hewed a great many into the afterlife, until, exhausted and outflanked, he leapt overboard and vanished into the sea, a defiant end that would inspire the *skalds* and singers for centuries.

FOR:

MADAME MINNA (D. 1096) . . .

. . . a prosperous and devout citizen in the Rhineland, who, cornered by a mob driven mad by the canard that local Jews had poisoned a well, would not accede to baptism or renounce her God, and true to the Judaic precept of *kiddush hashem*, chose to suffer the mortal insults to her merely physical body with the words "Delay no more."

FOR:

YORIMASA (D. 1180) . . .

. . . leader of the Minamoto clan at the first Battle of Uji who, pierced by an arrow and unable to marshal the further defense of the Byodo-in temple, quickly composed a regretful poem on the back of his war fan, and then, to confound the swarming foe intent on capturing and dishonouring him, opened his abdomen with his own blade to set his spirit free.

FOR:

ZAFAR KHAN (D. 1299) . . .

. . . lauded warrior of the Delhi Sultanate who, having been encircled by the Mongol horsemen he'd avidly pursued on the field, and having then spurned their offers of prestige and riches if he would only defect to their side, chose to die fighting as his realm's loyal champion, far from the frenzied shouts of his stranded infantry and the useless splendour of his caparisoned war elephants.

THIS IS FOR:

CONSTANTINE XI PALAIOLOGOS (D. 1453) . . .

. . . the last Byzantine emperor, who, on the fifty-fifth day of inspired and daring resistance against the Ottoman siege, seeing that the walls of his beloved Constantinople had finally fallen and vowing to share in its fate, divested himself of his imperial finery, rallied his doomed compatriots at the breach, and was hacked down by the swords of the sultan's slave soldiers.

FOR:

CHALCUCHIMAC (D. 1533) . . .

. . . renegade general of the disintegrating Incan Empire, who, captured by conquistadores near his mountain fastness, refused to convert to his captors' incomprehensible religion of love, and, as he was set alight, called on Viracocha, the creator god of his homeland, to exact vengeance for the calamities visited upon him and his people.

FOR:

GIORDANO BRUNO (D. 1600) . . .

. . . cosmologist and heretic, believer in an infinite universe with uncountable suns and planets, who, even after eight years' imprisonment would not recant his outlandish ideas, and told the Inquisitor before being hung upside down and burned naked at the stake, "Perhaps you pronounce this sentence against me with greater fear than I receive it."

FOR:

SIR WALTER RALEIGH (D. 1618) . . .

. . . poet, soldier, explorer, courtier, and one of England's first smokers (a man not dedicated to a long life of ease and safety) who, having provoked the lethal displeasure of his monarch, knelt at the chopping block and observed that the executioner's axe was "a Physician for all diseases and miseries" before urging its wielder to "Strike, man, strike!"

FOR:

JEAN-BAPTISTE POQUELIN
(D. 1673) . . .

. . . the tubercular playwright and actor better known as Molière, who, with admirable devotion to his audience (and, no doubt, a grasp on the compounding ironies of his situation) insisted on finishing his performance in *The Imaginary Invalid* after collapsing on stage from a pulmonary hemorrhage, only to expire hours later, a farceur trapped in a real-life tragedy.

THIS IS FOR:

GILES COREY (D. 1692) . . .

. . . an elderly, ornery farmer in Salem who, accused of witchcraft by his hysterical and covetous neighbours, did not deign to respond to the charges, and while later being crushed beneath a fiendish torture device to extract from him a plea, would say to the authorities only, "More weight," before dying an obstinate but unconvicted man.

FOR:

'GENTLEMAN JACK' SHEPPARD (D. 1724) . . .

. . . pickpocket, burglar, ingenious jail-breaker, and wisecracking fop who, apprehended by the law at last and escorted under heavy guard to the Tyburn gallows (stopping along the way for a pint of sherry in an Oxford Street tavern), was hung before a throng of 200,000 celebrants and fans, amidst stacks of his bestselling biography.

FOR:

DAVID HUME (D. 1776) . . .

. . corpulent gourmand, keen whist player, gentle friend, eloquent destroyer of superstitious dogmas, who entertained guests throughout his humiliating bed-ridden decline with droll humour and lucid self-scrutiny, never hedging his final bet by embracing the Almighty he previously won infamy for scorning.

FOR:

MARIE-JEANNE 'MANON' ROLAND (D. 1793) . . .

. . . pamphleteer and salonnière arrested during the Great Terror, who deftly argued her innocence before the haranguing ideologues of the Revolutionary Tribunal, went calmly to the guillotine (while comforting a condemned forger who shared her cart), and left behind, in a written pledge: "The tyrants may well oppress me, but demean me? Never."

FOR:

A WOMAN (D. 1803) . . .

. . . chattel, her name lost to us, who, caught in France's horrifying reprisals to impose order on its colony during the Haitian Revolution, turned to her virgin daughters as they were all prodded up to the scaffold and said, with a remorseless equanimity that emboldened the corralled onlookers and chilled their masters, "Be glad you will not be the mother of slaves."

THIS IS FOR:

SHATEYARONYAH (D. 1810) . . .

. . . the Wyandot warrior and elder known as 'Leatherlips' who, having dispassionately accepted news of his proscription by his more powerful rival, Tecumseh, retired to his wigwam for ablutions and a final meal, re-emerged in face paint and regalia, chanted his death song, and then awaited the release promised by a plummeting tomahawk.

FOR:

OWEN COFFIN (D. 1820) . . .

. . . the teenaged sailor from Nantucket, adrift in the Pacific Ocean for over three months after his ship had been rammed and sunk by a sperm whale, who, with pragmatic simplicity and a sense of fair play, consented to a fatal shot from a sidearm so that his flesh might nourish and sustain his emaciated crewmates.

FOR:

MOLLY MORGAN (D. 1835) . . .

. . . the rat-catcher's daughter, an arsonist, bigamist, and incorrigible flirt, banished by penal transport to Australia for stealing a few shillings' worth of yarn, who, having won parole, amassed lands and esteem through her industry, and departed having given away her estate to indigents that were just as desperate as she had been fifty years earlier.

FOR:

THOMAS FLETCHER (D. 1854) . . .

. . . private with the 4th Light Dragoons who, having charged the Russian artillery at Balaclava with the famed Six Hundred, and having been unhorsed by an enfilade of shot to the head that would later kill him, knelt alongside another crippled cavalryman and said "Get on my back, chum!", then bore the stranger from the welter of the field.

FOR:

ANNIE COOK (D. 1878) . . .

. . . proprietress of the Mansion House bordello, who, when a Yellow Fever epidemic erupted across the sweltering city of Memphis, transfigured her plush and gilded precincts into a field hospital, and ministered to its patients amidst the piteous moans and vomitous filth until she was claimed by the same contagion from which she had delivered so many of her neighbours.

THIS IS FOR:

NANSICA (D. 1890) . . .

. . . *ahosi* soldier of the Dahomey Kingdom (or simply 'Amazon' to astounded outlanders), who stormed the stockades and wetted her machete at the Battle of Cotonou, but whose woolen skullcap, flowered vest, and magic fetishes could not protect her from the bayoneted rifles of the European invader, or the exploding shells flung by his offshore gunboats.

FOR:

GURMUKH SINGH (D. 1897) . . .

. . . infantryman with India's 36th Sikhs who, having ignored all enticements to surrender to the ten thousand Pashtun tribesmen assaulting his Saragarhi hill fort, and having seen all twenty of his fellow defenders killed in a desperate mêlée, mounted such a savage and costly resistance that the attackers were finally forced to torch his building rather than face him in open combat.

FOR:

MARY ROGERS (D. 1899) . . .

. . . stewardess aboard the *Stella*, and a woman already widowed by the sea, who bequeathed her own lifebelt to a passenger when their steamship was impaled upon a reef, refused to board a lifeboat (lest her additional weight imperil the already teeming craft), and said, plainly, "Lord save me" before being dragged into the impartial depths.

FOR:

LAWRENCE 'TITUS' OATES
(D. 1912) . . .

. . . Captain with the Terra Nova Expedition who, afflicted by the frostbite that had rendered his feet a gangrenous slurry (and anguished by the knowledge that his ailing comrades might reach safety faster without him), took his leave from the camp tent with the words "I may be some time," and disappeared into the obliterating snow of an Antarctic blizzard.

FOR:

PATRICK VINCENT COLEMAN
(D. 1917) . . .

. . . husband, father of four, and train dispatcher in Halifax, Nova Scotia, who, having rejected orders to flee his office as a drifting munitions freighter caught fire in the adjacent harbour, spent his final minutes tapping out a telegrammed directive to halt incoming rail traffic, before being engulfed by a supersonic shock wave thick with fragmented glass, molten shrapnel, and human debris.

THIS IS FOR:

BRUCE FREDERICK CUMMINGS
(D. 1919) . . .

. . . naturalist, pastry fiend, multiple sclerosis sufferer, and slyly pseudonymous author behind *The Journal of a Disappointed Man*, who poked fun at his own infirmity and filled the ward with rackety good-natured mirth when his nurse struggled to maneuver his skewed and moribund physique upon the tangled sheets of his hospice bed.

FOR:

FRANK HAYES (D. 1923) . . .

. . . horse trainer, stableman, and one-time jockey in the Belmont Park steeplechase who, with otherworldly will (plus a touch of lucky happenstance), bucked the 20-1 odds against him, and resplendent in his racing silks, guided his thoroughbred to victory with nerveless fingers at the reins, having breathed his last before surging across the finish line.

FOR:

TUPUA TAMESESE LEALOFI III
(D. 1929)

. . . leader of the Mau independence movement, who abjured his people's proud martial ethos while guiding them to self-determination, and instructed his keening followers as he lay dying from a policeman's bullet to the back, "My blood has been spilt for Samoa. I am proud to give it. Do not dream of avenging it . . ."

FOR:

BEBEL GARCÍA (D. 1936) . . .

. . . soccer player for Deportivo de La Coruña and member of the Young Socialists, who, facing a firing squad of nationalists in the chaotic first days of Spain's civil war, held up an admonishing hand, and then, with the ribald insolence of youth, opened his buttoned fly and directed a contemptuous piss in his murderers' direction before giving them the nod to proceed.

FOR:

STEFANIA WILCZYŃSKA
(D. 1942) . .

. . . educator and surrogate mother who, refusing to forsake the 192 Warsaw Ghetto orphans in her care (despite multiple offers of escape and reprieve), succoured the children and accompanied them, with their faded toys and fretful questions, all the way to the gas chambers of Treblinka.

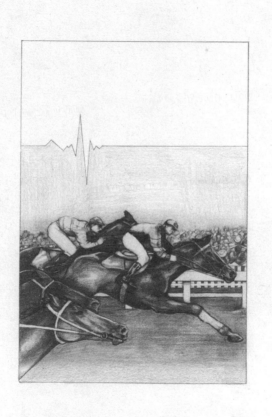

THIS IS FOR:

DANUTA 'INKA' SIEDZIKÓWNA
(D. 1946) . . .

. . . medical orderly with the anti-communist underground who, having held to her silence under torture by UB operatives, and having refused a blindfold at her execution, fixed a condemnatory gaze upon the Stalinist quislings arrayed to shoot her and shouted "Long Live Poland!" at the fatal moment, six days before her eighteenth birthday.

FOR:

THICH QUANG DUC (D. 1963) . . .

. . . Mahayana monk who, determined to provoke international scrutiny of the Catholic regime violently oppressing Buddhists in South Vietnam, assumed the lotus position in a busy Saigon intersection, was anointed with gasoline, and self-immolated in a protest all the more profound for the stunning silence with which it was conducted.

FOR:

LOUIS WASHKANSKY (D. 1967) . . .

. . . South African grocer, and the louche, irrepressible, scrappy recipient of the world's first human heart transplant, who clung to life for eighteen days after the procedure, through the terror of the unknown and the grueling guesswork of his physicians, so that the domains of medical science might be expanded and multitudes after him might realize true resurrection.

FOR:

ALEKSANDR GRIGORYEVICH
LELECHENKO (D. 1986) . . .

. . . electrical engineer who, mindful of pre-
serving his younger colleagues' lives during the
first frantic efforts to mitigate the Chernobyl
disaster, himself waded into waters boiling with
fission's invisible inferno in order to disable
pumps and generators, until he succumbed to
the agonies of acute radiation sickness.

FOR:

ADMIRA ISMIĆ AND BOŠKO BRKIĆ (D. 1993) . . .

. . . she a Bosniak Muslim and he an Orthodox Serb, who, buoyed by their ardency and juvenescence, hazarded a flight from besieged Sarajevo together across the deadly Vrbanja Bridge and, felled by a sniper, reposed in a tender embrace, their invincible love a rebuke to those factions that would see their country riven by ethnic hate.

THIS IS FOR:

CYRIL RICHARD RESCORLA
(D. 2001) . . .

. . . veteran, security expert, far-flung Cornish-man, who led thousands of evacuees safely from the stricken World Trade Center's South Tower (singing jaunty anthems and folk songs to allay their fears) before re-entering the building one time too many and being consumed in the tumbling conflagration.

FOR:

LIVIU LIBRESCU (D. 2007) . . .

. . . aeronautics specialist, Holocaust survivor, and professor at Virginia Polytechnic University, who barred the door to his lecture hall when a gun-laden madman stalked the corridors of the school, and interposed his body between the spray of bullets and the wildly veering pupils in his charge so that some of them might escape through the windows nearby.

FOR:

KHALED AL-ASAAD (D. 2015) . . .

. . . Syrian archaeologist and curator, who, determined to safeguard the ancient city of Palmyra's priceless cultural bequest to humanity, refused to betray the location of hidden relics to looting Islamists beguiled by a fever dream of Heaven-sanctioned omnipotence, and was beheaded in a public square before the gloating faces of the pious.

FOR:

BERTA CÁCERES (D. 2016) . . .

. . . Honduran environmentalist and Indigenous leader, who for years braved slanders, assaults, death threats, and vexatious lawsuits while obstructing the erection of a dam on annexed land, and who, when the promised hit squad came and staved in the door of her home, raked her nails at the closest *sicario* as he fired three rounds into her unruly and obdurate person.

A SMALL BOOK OF EXEMPLARY DEATHS

FOR:

NIC AND TREES ELDERHORST
(D. 2017) . . .

. . . wed at the mid-point of the calamitous twentieth century, who, together at the age of ninety-one, he dwindling from a stroke, she discomposed by the insidious erasures of dementia, reached boldly for the exit, and were euthanized hand in hand, their departure punctuated with a kiss.

NOTES

1. The fame of Dienekes, one of 300 Spartan peers charged with defending the Hot Gates mountain pass from an overwhelming force of invading Persians, is second only to that of his king, Leonidas. Both of them, and virtually all of their compatriots, were wiped out in a suicidal rearguard action, along with their helot slaves and a smattering of Thespian and Theban allies. The Persians occupied parts of central Greece in the aftermath of the battle and razed Athens, before a large allied force of Greek city states expelled them the following year.

2. According to the historian Herodotus (484 BCE-425 BCE), Leonidas excused Aristodemus and another Spartan hoplite named Eurytus from battle

at Thermopylae, as both had been virtually blinded by the same eye complaint. Eurytus hurled himself into the fray and was killed, his fidelity to the Spartan code only serving to compound Aristodemus' shame when he returned home. Another Spartan inadvertently survived Thermopylae as well, a man named Pantites who'd been sent away on a diplomatic mission in Thessaly, who hung himself shortly thereafter, unable to live with the disgrace of having missed the battle.

3. The comically ugly Socrates, progenitor of the Western philosophical tradition, contended that the little wisdom he possessed derived from acknowledging the vastness of his own ignorance. Forever pestering statesmen and other thinkers with irksome questions about what constituted justice, goodness, and truth, he was eventually brought to trial and convicted of impiety and corrupting the minds of Athens' young. According to two of his disciples, Xenophon and Plato, Socrates had ample opportunity to escape his execution but elected not to.

4. The Sacred Band of Thebes, operational through most of the fourth century BCE, was comprised of soldiers, typically between the ages of twenty and thirty, who were selected for their martial prowess and merit.

The fact that the fighting unit consisted of homosexual pairs was believed to enhance the cohesion and mutually reinforcing courage of its members. It was annihilated when Philip's Macedonian army crushed the loose alliance of fractious and exhausted city states defying him, and he effectively became hegemon of Greece. Philip's precocious teenaged son, Alexander (later The Great), is believed to have led that portion of the Macedonian phalanx (or possibly cavalry) that first broke the ranks of the Sacred Band.

5. Sophonisba fell into Roman hands after the Battle of Bagbades in North Africa, when the legions of Publius Cornelius Scipio scattered a Carthaginian army commanded by Sophonisba's father, Hasdrubal Gisco. The war conclude within a year, when Scipio defeated the forces of Hannibal at Zama, and Carthage was neutralized militarily and made to pay reparations to Rome.

6. The Battle of Thapsus (in modern-day Tunisia) was a catastrophe for the Optimates–the senatorial faction determined to preserve Rome as a republic and oppose Julius Caesar's ascent to virtually unlimited power. Cato the Younger, one of Caesar's most unremitting foes, committed suicide after the failed engagement;

Pompey had already been defeated and murdered a couple of years earlier, and Cicero, who never took to the field but was a vocal critic of Caesar's actions, was effectively muzzled back in Rome. Caesar would go on to be appointed dictator in perpetuity, and was later deified; Rome would remain an Empire thereafter, to be ruled by a succession of emperors.

7.   The assassination plot against Nero was started by the statesman, Gaius Calpurnius Piso, who hoped to become emperor in his stead, and involved a number of conspirators from Rome's senatorial and equestrian classes, as well as centurions and the Praetorian Guard. The plot was discovered when a ship's captain was invited to participate in the subterfuge, and instead informed Nero, hoping to win favour. In the ensuing investigation, some of Rome's elite men quickly confessed their guilt or begged for clemency without being tortured at all; Epicharis held firm and strangled herself from the back of a chair with her own girdle. When the paranoid Nero later commenced a purge of his court, the Stoic philosopher Seneca, the poet Lucan, and Petronius (believed to be the author of *The Satyricon*) were all ordered to commit suicide.

8. The verifiable details of Hua Tuo's life have been partially obscured by fanciful embellishment over the years. Like some of the other great names of his age (including his nemesis, Cao Cao) he appears as a fictionalized character in the classic Chinese historical novel sequence, *Romance of the Three Kingdoms*, as well as various folkloric and oral traditions. Accounts by his associates and disciples all dwell on his precocious medical expertise, and he was evidently a pioneer in the effective use of anaesthesia (his concoction involved the pharmacological properties of wine and cannabis, or possibly opium), which he used prior to performing invasive surgical procedures. While incarcerated, Hua Tuo set down on a scroll an explication of the esoteric medical techniques he'd devised over the course of his career, and on the day of his execution, handed it to a guard for posterity's sake. The fearful man refused to pass it on to his superiors, and the invaluable treatise was burned instead.

9. Hypatia lived in that tumultuous period when pagan beliefs and rituals in the Mediterranean world were being forced aside by a newly powerful Christianity. For so long the faith of a persecuted minority, it was

now in the ascendant, and its adherents frequently militated against rival groups that had previously scorned it. In the years leading up to Hypatia's murder, Christian mobs had attacked Alexandria's great library, destroyed synagogues, and expelled the Jews. According to contemporaries, Hypatia was a dazzling orator who welcomed earnest pupils of any background. The city's patriarch, Cyril, keen to extinguish any philosophy at variance from Christ's supposed teachings, wielded a group of violent true believers, the *parabalani*, with great ruthlessness, and it is they who tore Hypatia from her carriage on the way to the auditorium and carved her to pieces with shells and shards of pottery. Ironically, the Neoplatonic creed she adhered to was not unlike Christianity in its contempt for the body, and she submitted to her brutal end with composure.

10. 'Kanarang' was the title given to a warden or governor charged with protecting the frontier of The Sassanid (or Neo-Persian) Empire. Adurgundbad had been awarded the high office for his impressive soldiering career, and for helping Kavad I win his throne after a bloody dynastic struggle. Kavad's successor, Khosrow,

faced similar difficulties surrounding his royal claim; his order to eliminate any rivals, in this case, his young nephew, came after the quashing of a dangerous plot by would-be usurpers. Alas, Adurgundhad's admirable deed was nearly vitiated by his own son, who, no doubt motivated by a potent mixture of terror and greed, betrayed him to the king and saw him executed. The boy at the centre of all this intrigue is thought to have found asylum in the court of Persia's arch-rival, Byzantium, after which he disappears from history.

11. Even after the death of Muhammad in 632, Arab Muslim armies continued their rapid expansion through neighbouring areas, bringing religious conversion by fire and sword to the peoples of Mesopotamia, Syria, Egypt, Iran, and Afghanistan. The conquest of the Maghreb (Northwest Africa) commenced in 647, and dragged on for decades. It's thought that Dihya, probably a Christian (or, less likely, a Judaized) Berber rallied the tribes of the region, and inflicted a stinging defeat on the Arabs at the Battle of Meskiana in 698. But the ineluctable Arab advance resumed five years later, and Dihya's uprising was quashed, resulting in her violent death and the eventual Islamification of the region.

12. Many of the details surrounding Trygvasson's life, derived as they are from Icelandic sagas, are apocryphal, if not outright fiction. Still, the sources agree on these points: that his father was murdered around the time of his birth, and that he led a fugitive existence with his mother for his first few years; that, as a boy, he was captured by Estonian seafarers and sold into slavery; that he eventually entered into military service under Vladimir the Great of Kiev, where he won renown for his exploits; and that after years of raiding, a few politically advantageous marriages, and a conversion to Christianity, he ousted the unpopular Jarl Haakon of Norway, and became king there. His zealous brutality won him many determined enemies; a combined force of Wendish, Swedish, and Danish fleets, plus Haakon's vengeful sons, killed Trygvasson at the Battle of Svolder, on the Baltic Sea.

13. Madame Minna was just one victim of the Worms Massacre, where at least 800 German Jews were murdered, and many more beaten, terrorized, driven to suicide, or forcibly baptized. The Rhineland, and much of Europe, had been whipped into a lunatic fervour by Pope Urban II's call for a crusade to seize the

Holy Land from Muslim possession. And such was the impatience to expunge the infidel that some Christians began by attacking those in their midst. Minna was well-connected with the nobility of the town, but these connections were not enough to save her, and her relative wealth probably increased her attractiveness as a target.

14. Yorimasa Minamoto's is the first recorded instance of a samurai committing *hara kiri* or *seppuku* (ritual suicide by disembowelment) in response to an impending military defeat, though the act itself was already integral to Japanese society as a means of expiating one's failures or sins and restoring one's honour. His performance was deemed so estimable that it became the template for later samurai caught in similar predicaments. (Indeed, nearly four centuries later, Akechi Mitsutoshi may have outperformed his progenitor by writing *his* poem on a wall, using a brush dipped in the blood of his own abdomen.) A war fan often had blades, and could be relied upon as a weapon of last resort, but was also used to signal troops and shield one's eyes from the sun's glare. Yorimasa's poem read as follows: *Like a fossil tree/From which we gather no flowers/Sad has been my life/Fated no fruit to produce.*

15. The Delhi Sultanate was an empire that, at its peak, covered most of the Indian subcontinent, and had been created when Islamized Turks had swept southwards from the Central Asian steppes, conquering various Hindu and Buddhist kingdoms in the early thirteenth century. Nearly a century later, northern and central India were firmly under Muslim control, but by then the sultanate faced invasion itself from Mongol armies led by the successors of that great conqueror, Genghis. Zafar Khan (known also as Hizabruddin) had already won fame by defeating the Mongols twice in earlier engagements, but at the Battle of Kili, he and his cavalry were tricked into chasing the feigned retreat of the enemy, and, cut off from any assistance or escape route, were killed. His master, Sultan Alauddin Khalji, incensed by Khan's tactical error, and jealous of the fame as a martial hero, had his name erased from many of the official chronicles.

16. By 1453, the Byzantine Empire was tottering on the edge of collapse, and its mighty capital, Constantinople, had fallen into disrepair, with its population much reduced by plague and internecine wars with encroaching neighbours. When the youthful and ambitious

Sultan Mehmed II began mustering his vast army for invasion, Emperor Constantine, anticipating a conflict of nearly eschatological import, requested reinforcements from the Latin kingdoms to the west, but very few heeded his call; in the end, a mere 7000 defenders manned the walls against a besieging force of perhaps 80,000. The battle itself was full of strategic and technological marvels: unprecedentedly massive cannons, elaborate sapping operations and tunnel warfare, the smuggling of a fleet of ships across dry land to circumvent defenses in the city's harbour. Constantinople's fall was tantamount to the end of the Roman Empire; Constantine's body was never identified.

17. Chalcuchimac was one of the ablest Incan generals at the time of the Spanish invasion, and won a number of victories over the (admittedly outnumbered) conquistadores before he was apprehended. He was loyal to Atahualpa, the last true Incan emperor, who himself had been captured by a tiny Spanish force in his own capital, robbed of his vast royal treasury, subjected to a show trial for idolatry and other offences, and then garroted. Chalcuchimac was offered a quick death if he converted to Catholicism beforehand and

submitted to baptism, but he refused. Instead, he was burned alive, an excruciation for anyone, but particularly fearsome for Incans, as they believed their souls could not depart from a scorched body to reach the afterlife.

18. Arrogant, impatient, and disdainful of his intellectual inferiors, Giordano Bruno was probably an unpleasant man with whom to spend one's time, but his place in history's pantheon of scientific freethinkers is secure, even if he is not much read today. Trained in the Dominican Order, and made an ordained priest in his early twenties, Bruno was prone to making unrestrained philosophical speculations that won him opprobrium from his betters, and he was forced to lead a precarious and peripatetic existence. His theories on heliocentrism and the existence of other suns and worlds (which he posited might also support life) were bad enough in the eyes of the Church, but it was probably his doubts surrounding transubstantiation and the divinity of Christ that sealed his fate. He was executed in the Campo de' Fiori. Authorities then tossed Bruno's remains in the Tiber river, which was a failed attempt at his total erasure.

19. Raleigh's large and multifarious talents were sometimes outstripped by his heedlessness and eruptions of bad luck. Elizabeth I had him imprisoned in the Tower of London when she learned that he had seduced and secretly married one of her ladies-in-waiting. Elizabeth's successor, James I, had him reacquainted with the Tower a few years later, when Raleigh was implicated in a plot to remove the new king from power, quite possibly a baseless charge, but one that imperiled Raleigh's social and political standing. When men from Raleigh's expeditionary force in Guyana illegally attacked a Spanish outpost, Raleigh himself was called to account in London; diplomatic pressure from Spain ensured that he would pay with his life. He left a tobacco pouch behind in his prison cell, a token from his years adventuring in the New World.

20. Molière's prolificacy and mastery of many forms makes him as much a colossus in French letters as Shakespeare in English. But he was an accomplished actor and musician as well, having honed his skills with an itinerant theatre troupe as a youth. At the peak of his fame, he enjoyed the patronage and protection of Louis XIV, and just as well, because his work often targeted and outraged

the nobility and the clergy, who campaigned to have his plays banned. On the night of his death, loved ones concerned by his deteriorating health pleaded with him to cancel his performance, but he carried on; even after his onstage collapse, he acted to the play's conclusion, but a violent and irresistible coughing fit afterwards burst a vessel, and he bled to death. As an actor he was denied a burial in consecrated ground, but his remains have since been moved to precincts more fitting to one of his influence and achievement.

21. Well, unconvicted of witchcraft, anyway. Records show that Giles Corey had, years earlier, beaten one of his farm workers with excessive force, which had resulted in the man's death, a crime for which he was found guilty and fined. But where the later superstitious nonsense was concerned, Corey refused to plead, aware that he could not be tried until he had asserted whether he was guilty of the charges or not. The court's remedy, *peine forte et dure* or 'pressing', entailed placing heavy stones and iron on the defendant until pain and suffocation forced him or her to acquiesce. Corey never did, choosing instead to taunt and stymie his torturers for more than two days until he died.

Three women were arrested for witchcraft the same day Corey was, and, in the ensuing madness, his own wife, Martha, was hung for the same imaginary crime.

22. Jack Sheppard got his start in life as a carpenter's apprentice, but he soon fell in with a crew of scapegraces and prostitutes at his local tavern who introduced him to the excitements and remunerations of life in the criminal underworld. He started small, shoplifting and fencing stolen goods, before moving on to burglary and even a brief stint as a highwayman. Diminutive, witty, and charismatic, he became celebrated for his astonishing prison breaks, lock-picking his manacles, wriggling through iron bars, and abseiling from windows with knotted bedclothes. During those stretches when he was incarcerated, his jailers would charge members of the public to come gawk at their famed prisoner. Resourceful to the last, Sheppard planned to cut through his ropes on the way to the gallows, but this gambit failed when a prison warder confiscated his hidden penknife. His autobiography, it's believed, was ghostwritten by an admiring (and business-minded) Daniel Defoe.

23. Even in a city such as Edinburgh, a great centre of eighteenth-century Enlightenment, David Hume stood

out as a prodigy. By the age of ten, he was enrolled in university, studying Greek, Latin, metaphysics, and logic, and by his late twenties he had already penned his *Treatises*, a hugely ambitious attempt to lay the foundations for a new understanding of human behaviour (without, scandalously, any appeal to a Higher Power). He often clashed with other titans of the age (James Boswell was confounded by Hume's placid unbelief in a Christian afterlife, while the sterner Samuel Johnson thought such a view was depraved), but nearly all his contemporaries noted his kindly and jocund demeanor, with Adam Smith identifying him as close to 'a perfectly wise and virtuous man, as perhaps the nature of human frailty will permit.' (That vaunted wisdom, it's true, was nowhere in evidence on those few occasions when Hume was prompted to give his depressingly conventional views on race; genius though he might have been, he wasn't clever enough to hold informed twenty-first century views in his little corner of eighteenth-century Europe.) He died, messily, of abdominal cancer, having been weakened by bloody incontinence for weeks beforehand, but his good humour never deserted him.

24. Madame Roland was a member of the Girondins, an alliance of politically active intellectuals and pamphleteers who sought the eventual abolition of the French monarchy. Deemed insufficiently radical in their views and methods during the Revolution by their more ruthless rivals, the Montagnards, they were hunted down and purged during the Terror's hideous apotheosis. Roland herself was seemingly unflappable to the end, and declaimed at the scaffold the immortal line, 'O freedom, what crimes are committed in your name!', even as the incensed sans-culottes chanted abuse. Her heartsick husband, upon hearing of her death from his exile in the countryside, committed suicide; her confidant and possible lover, Francois Buzot, followed suit a few months later. She wrote her memoirs in prison, from which her pledge about tyrants is drawn.

25. The Haitian Revolution in the French colony once known as Saint-Domingue was a brutal and sanguinary conflict; white slaveholders, black slaves, and the mulattoes they alternately spurned and allied themselves with all inflicted horrific cruelties upon one another. Rape, mutilation, and the beheading

of children were employed tactically to terrorize the enemy. Efforts to suppress the revolt by colonial authorities were exceedingly barbarous. Stories of slaves being eaten alive by dogs or roasted over pits were not uncommon. But such barbarity often undermined their efforts to quell dissent. Slaves endured their torments with such fortitude it ultimately demoralized the perpetrators. The leader of the revolt, Toussaint Louverture, emerged victorious after five years, though by then the war had become complicated by Spanish and British forces advancing their own interests in the Caribbean.

26. The Wyandots were a confederacy of Iroquois-speaking tribes who had traditionally inhabited what is now southern Ontario in Canada, but who, by the early nineteenth-century, had been displaced into parts of the USA by infectious disease and armed conflict. Chief Shateyaronyah (known as 'Leatherlips', because of his reputation for keeping his word), advocated peaceful co-existence with the seemingly unstoppable surge of White settlers, seeing no viable alternative, and signed a treaty that ceded to them parts of modern-day Ohio. Tecumseh, a Shawnee chief at the head

of a large pan-tribal alliance, was of a much more militaristic bent; he viewed Shateyaronyah's behaviour as dangerously accommodationist and had him executed before embarking on a war with the American army. Three years later, Tecumseh was dead too, killed in battle, with his alliance collapsed, and its many constituent peoples herded onto reserves.

27. The lost crewmen of the *Essex* ended up eating seven of their fellows before the survivors were rescued, with nearly all the cannibalism confined to the bodies of those who had died of starvation, thirst, or exposure. But circumstances had grown so mortally desperate on Coffin's drifting whaleboat that the men decided to draw lots to see who would be sacrificed for the good of the group. When it was revealed that Coffin had been selected, Captain George Pollard (Coffin's protective older cousin) urged the others to reconsider, or to accept him as a substitute. Coffin, however, insisted that the results be honoured, and he gamely submitted to his fate. His unlucky friend, Charles Ramsdell, after losing another drawing of lots, was made to act as executioner.

28. While she's now celebrated as one of the more remarkable rapscallions in Australian history, Molly

Morgan was born in Shropshire, and was living a life of semi-respectable domesticity with a husband and two children at the time of her initial arrest. Her first voyage to the penal colony in New South Wales was aboard the *Neptune*, a filthy and under-provisioned vessel that saw nearly half its convict occupants succumb to disease or starvation, but by seducing various crew members to win better rations, she survived the months-long ordeal without lasting physical detriment. She later escaped back to England aboard a store ship (briefly becoming the captain's mistress) and settled in Plymouth where she wed, illegitimately, another man, suffering a miserable union for a time before allegedly burning down his house and being banished to Australia once again. In her closing years, having wed a third time and become a prosperous farmer and inn-keeper, she helped to finance a school and a hospital, used her influence to argue for clemency on behalf of condemned criminals, and shared her largesse with the poor and unready in a hostile land.

29. Thomas Fletcher was a member of the British Light Brigade which, during the Crimean War at the Battle

of Balaclava, made a disastrous frontal assault on a battery of Russian guns, a task for which it was tactically ill-suited. The light cavalry was armed primarily with lances and sabres, and had to cover a large distance through a valley under incessant fire from all sides before it reached its intended target and engaged the Russian gunners and infantry in combat. The brigade suffered a 40 per cent casualty rate during the action, and more than half of its horses were killed, all because of a miscommunication in the chain of command. Alfred, Lord Tennyson's famous poem about the charge captures some of the confusion, slaughter, and unquestioning (or fatalistic) gallantry that marked the engagement. Fletcher's actions were recorded by the man he rescued, Private James Wightman of the 17th Lancers.

30. Yellow Fever originated in Africa and is thought to have been introduced to the Americas by transatlantic slave ships. Epidemics were first reported in the Caribbean in the mid-1600s, with the virus then proliferating to other warm and humid regions where mosquitoes, the transmitters of the disease, thrive. The Lower Mississippi valley suffered through multiple outbreaks in the 1800s, but the one in 1878 exacted the highest

death toll. Annie Cook (probably her working name) had survived a previous outbreak in 1873, but in this instance exhaustion and constant proximity to the afflicted in her makeshift hospital tilted the odds against her. In the aftermath, there were many condescending homilies in newspapers and church groups about the "fallen woman" spiritually cleansed by her sacrifice (even Cook's headstone compares her to the biblical Mary Magdalene), but nothing can detract from her obvious and unswerving dedication to her fellow Memphis citizens.

31. Centuries of rapine and subjugation, as practiced by the European powers, blight the pages of nearly any history of Africa one cares to read. But it's worth remembering that, even during the colonial era, the continent spawned a substantial number of homegrown dynasties that were extremely bellicose and expansionist in nature. The Dahomey Kingdom (in what is now Benin) was one such example; its people, the Fon, waged almost continuous war on their neighbours, selling thousands of their captives to European and Muslim slavers in return for alcohol, tobacco, or firearms. What made the burgeoning empire even more

striking was its ruthless all-female corps of soldiers, the *ahosi* ("king's wives") or *mino* ("our mothers"), whose ferocity and skill with musket, club, and machete surpassed that of their male counterparts. The imperial ambitions of the Dahomey eventually bumped up against the even grander ones of France, and were dashed in several attritional campaigns. Nansica had been inducted into her cruel sisterhood a few months before the fatal battle, and was still a youth. She was a terror to her enemies, but a prisoner, too, of a culture stuck in the insane logic of perpetual aggression.

32. The Battle of Saragarhi was fought in The North-West Frontier Province of British India, in what is now Pakistan. Britain had long maintained a military presence there to check the influence of the Russian Empire in neighbouring Afghanistan, but the 36th Sikhs was quite a new infantry regiment, and most of the twenty-one men involved in the hill-fort siege had only just been stationed there as reinforcements after a nearby fort had been attacked. The battle was part of a larger Pashtun insurgency against British rule, led by Afridi and Orkzai tribes, which would be put down the following year. Details of the conflict were relayed

in real time to nearby British forces by means of a heliograph communications device. All of the defenders were posthumously awarded the Indian Order of Merit, the highest military honour available.

33. The *Stella* was a ferry that travelled between Southampton and the islands in the English Channel. It strayed off course in the fog, collided with a submerged sandstone shelf known as The Casquets, and sank within minutes (its demise hastened by its exploding boilers), taking with it the lives of 105 people. Witnesses agreed that all the crew members' behaviour was exemplary, but Rogers was particularly praised for so calmly and unselfishly seeing to the safety of the passengers in her care. She had three dependents at the time of her death (a daughter, son, and elderly father) but a sympathetic public raised funds to support them in the aftermath of the tragedy. Her husband, while on another ship nineteen years earlier, had himself been washed overboard and drowned.

34. Robert Falcon Scott's Terra Nova expedition was largely successful from a scientific perspective, and it did reach the South Pole as intended (but was beaten there by Roald Amundsen's rival Norwegian team).

On the return trip, though, Scott and his men were punished by poor weather, injuries, frostbite, and possibly scurvy, which made their progress agonizing and far too slow relative to the provisions they were consuming. Oates had already been cited for conspicuous bravery during his years as a soldier in the Boer War, and this virtue did not desert him even as his body failed. His famous final words must surely rival Dienekes' quip, two-and-a-half millennia earlier, for their humour-tinged nonchalance, but his sacrifice was for naught. His comrades all perished a mere eleven miles from a large supply depot that might have saved them.

35. The Halifax Explosion was caused by the collision in the harbour of the *SS Imo*, a Norwegian steamship full of relief supplies for the Allied war effort, and the French *SS Mont-Blanc*, also Europe-bound, which contained thousands of tons of explosives, and which was ignited by the impact. 'Vince' Coleman was already something of a local celebrity for having leapt onto a runaway engine some months earlier, preventing a crash with another train. When a passing sailor screamed a warning, Coleman oversaw the quick

departure of his staff before returning to his telegraph to send his critical message, an act that probably saved upwards of 300 lives, and bore the poignant sign-off, "Guess this will be my last message. Good-bye, boys." The ensuing detonation, possibly the most devastating prior to the nuclear age, levelled thousands of buildings, triggered a tsunami, and strafed the city with secondary missiles, killing approximately 2,000 people and injuring entire generations of Haligonians. One of the iron deck cannons from the otherwise vapourized *Mont-Blanc* was eventually found about three miles away.

36. Cummings published his *Journal of a Disappointed Man* in 1919, with a slimmer follow-up volume of entries a year later. The books were released under the *nom de plume* W. N. P. Barbellion (created by combining the names of several wretched historical figures with the name of his favourite pastry shop), and were not just a record of the author's youthful excitations and animadversions, or of his consuming interest in the natural world, but of his rapid deterioration from the fatal demyelinating disease affecting his central nervous system. Some reviewers baulked at what

they perceived to be the unseemly candour of certain passages, but the critical reception overall was welcoming, and H. G. Wells provided the first book with an Introduction. Cummings died at the age of thirty, but his work endures in the canon as a minor classic, a moving portrait of an ebullient and talented character unfairly thwarted.

37. Poor Hayes undertook a drastic weight-cutting program in the days before the race, jogging and sweating away close to fifteen pounds without due regard for his health. It's thought that extreme dehydration (compounded, perhaps, by an electrolyte imbalance), plus the rigours of the race itself, led to his fatal heart attack near the end of the event. Some may debate the reasons for his inclusion here, arguing that it was little more than gravity or the involuntary clenchings of a failed nervous system that kept him in the saddle as he crossed the finish line. I'd prefer to believe that he was unwittingly adhering to an injunction found in the 18th-century samurai manual, *Hagakure*: "Even if one's head were to be suddenly cut off, he should be able to do one more action with certainty." That is to say, even with his heart stopped, Hayes, with his training,

resolute intention, and prodigious effort, guided his last moment to its triumphant conclusion. Alas, the winning horse, Sweet Kiss, never raced again.

38. The Mau movement campaigned for Samoan independence from colonial rule by means of civil disobedience and non-violent protest. Germany, the United Kingdom, and the United States had all variously vied for control of Samoa, but by 1929 Lealofi's homeland was under the mandate of New Zealand, whose lackadaisical efforts to contain the influenza outbreak there a decade earlier resulted in a shocking death toll among the population, and galvanized native resistance. On December 28, subsequently known as Black Saturday, Mau demonstrators were fired upon by police; eight people were killed (some of them while trying to shield Lealofi's body from further harm after he'd been felled by the initial salvo of bullets), and approximately fifty more were injured. It wasn't until 1962 that Samoa won its independence, but Lealofi's son would go on to serve two terms as prime minister in the country his father's death had helped emancipate.

39. Garcia was one of the earliest casualties of the Spanish Civil War, accosted in the purges that ensued

when fascist forces (assembled under their banner as 'Nationalists') rose up in a coup designed to remove Spain's legally elected (and left-leaning) Popular Front government from power. The coup was not immediately successful, and so the country descended into a three-year conflict that killed untold hundreds of thousands, and became a military training ground for a rapidly rearming Nazi Germany whose leaders were very much invested in the outcome of the struggle. Garcia was a recognizable figure because of his exploits on the soccer pitch, and he held opinions that were anathema to the Nationalists, so he became an obvious target as lawlessness and chaos engulfed the nation. He was only twenty-one when he died.

40. Wilczyńska was assistant to the famed educator and author, Dr. Janusz Korzack, who wrote several storybooks, and pedagogical manifestos about child-rearing and the rights of children. Shortly after Poland was invaded and occupied by Germany, the orphanage they had been running in Warsaw was forced to relocate to the Ghetto, a grim depot that imprisoned around 400,000 heavily surveilled and materially deprived Jews. In the summer of 1942, local authorities

implemented the so-called Kinder Aktion, part of a larger scheme to mass murder the area's inhabitants; witnesses report that Korzack and Wilczyńska, under armed guard, led nearly 200 children from the building to the train station in orderly, hand-holding rows, each of them neatly attired, and clutching a favourite possession. A Polish resistance group had offered to spirit the adults out of the Ghetto, and the Germans themselves may have even offered to send them to another, less lethal, concentration camp in Theresienstadt, where they might have lived to the end of the war, but they dismissed all offers, instead giving their young wards courage and comfort on their last day together.

41. There's some debate as to whether or not Danuta Siedzikówna was an actual combatant in her duties with the Polish Home Army, or whether she was merely a courier for supplies and intelligence. In the end, it didn't matter. Her country, having already suffered through the genocidal depredations of the Nazis, was subsequently locked in the iron grip of the Soviets, who were determined to extirpate all groups hostile to their utopian project. She was executed alongside

another, similarly courageous, anti-communist partisan named Feliks Selmanowicz, having joined the Home Army three years earlier after her mother had been murdered by the Gestapo.

42. Thich Quang Duc was not the first or the last Buddhist monk to resort to such an act. Self-immolation as a form of protest had been carried out in Vietnam before (and had been used in religious ceremonies as a sort of extreme reverencing of Gautama Buddha himself). More recently, it has been used by Tibetans to protest the Chinese occupation of their country–with such ubiquity, in fact, that senior figures there have started to condemn the practice. Nevertheless, Duc's sacrifice in 1963 shocked the world, and brought incredible pressure to bear on the country's Catholic President, Ngo Dinh Diem, who was later deposed in a coup.

43. Louis Washkansky had been physically formidable in his youth, but by his early fifties he was trapped in a rapidly failing body; congestive heart failure, liver and kidney failure, and dangerously impaired breathing had made his mere existence truly hellish. His physicians, led by Dr Christiaan Barnard, marveled at the state of his cardiac muscle, which was grossly oversized and

ravaged with scar tissue. Washkansky's contribution to humanity was made possible by the donor, Denise Darvall, whose young heart was granted a brief coda in another body, and for more than two weeks he gave media interviews, joked with hospital staff, and provided constant jocular reassurances to his wife. He died from a massive lung infection, probably enabled by the immunosuppressant drugs he'd been administered to reduce the odds of organ rejection. As of 2022, more than 3,500 heart transplants are successfully performed every year, and can add decades to a life.

44. Aleksandr Grigoryevich Lelechenko was one of thirty-one people whom the Soviet Union officially admitted had been killed by the Chernobyl meltdown in 1986. But the true number of fatalities, without a doubt, is in the thousands. The first of these were among 'the liquidators' (the men and women charged with cleaning up the resultant mess, sealing the disaster zone, and treating their injured or dying fellows), and then the Ukrainian and even general European populations afflicted by elevated rates of cancer for decades afterwards. Lelechenko was apparently exposed to 2,500 rad of radiation (which is more than

a lethal dose), and would have been overcome by nausea, vomiting, acute abdominal pain, and later, tissue ulceration and desquamation, so his decisive efforts are nothing short of astounding. He was posthumously awarded the Order of Lenin, the Union's highest civilian honour.

45. The wars that led to the breakup of Yugoslavia in the early 1990s were notable for their unusually high casualty rate among non-combatants. Concentration camps, forced resettlement, systemic rape as a means of intimidation and humiliation, and the execution of over 8,000 unarmed Muslim men and boys in Srebrenica alone finally provoked a military intervention by NATO forces in 1994, but it was too late for innocents like Ismić and Brkić . The young couple, both twenty-five-years-old and sweethearts since high school, had been granted permission to leave the city but were shot all the same. He was killed instantly, while she, in a terrible moment of pathos, crawled to his inert body and wrapped her arms around him as she bled out.

46. Born in Hayle, a small town in southwest England, Rescorla joined the British military in 1957 while

still a teen, and served with paratrooper and intelligence units in Cyprus. Later, he moved to New York, enlisted in the US Army, and became a platoon leader in Vietnam, where he received various medals for bravery and meritorious service. Having become adept at identifying and mitigating threats to human life, he parlayed his skills into a career in corporate security, ultimately working for Morgan Stanley in the World Trade Center. It was there, in 1997, that he stressed to his employers the susceptibility of the buildings to terrorist attack, and urged them to relocate their offices, a warning that went unheeded. On September 11, 2001, after the first plane struck the WTC North Tower, Rescorla disobeyed the Port Authority's directives and began evacuating nearly 2700 employees out of their offices. He was last spotted on the tenth floor of the burning South Tower, determined to leave only after the last living person had been escorted outside.

47. Before he was cut down on a verdant American campus, this apparently quiet and modest professor had already been subjected to the inhumanity of the modern era's most devastating totalitarianisms, and had emerged unbroken. Born in Romania, Liviu Librescu

was interred as a child in both a labour camp and a Jewish ghetto by Nazi collaborators during World War II. Later, as a young researcher and engineer, he was thrown into peril when he refused to swear allegiance to his country's Communist Party, and ultimately sought refuge in Israel. During his autumnal years, when he'd elected to take a position at Virginia Tech, he enjoyed a flourishing career, a late surge in productivity that was halted by the deranged actions of a deeply disturbed undergraduate student named Seung-Hui Cho. Librescu's sacrifice bought his class enough time to leap from the classroom's second-story windows and escape, though Minal Panchal, a foreign student from Mumbai, was slain by gunfire alongside him. In a ghastly coincidence, the massacre took place during Yom HaShoah, a day of commemoration for the millions murdered in the Holocaust.

48. The ancient city of Palmyra, located along the caravan routes of the Silk Road, bears the imprint of many mighty civilization–Mesopotamian, Persian, Greco-Roman, Byzantine, and Turco-Mongolian–but it reached the zenith of its prosperity and influence as a Roman *colonia* in the 3rd century. Asaad, who was born

in Palmyra, worked as the head of antiquities there for more than forty years, and was instrumental in getting it recognized by UNESCO as a World Heritage Site, was detained and tortured by ISIS jihadists searching for treasure they could illicitly sell to fund their war efforts. After being resolutely unhelpful for a month, he was publicly beheaded by a masked swordsman. Four years later, ISIS had been all but eradicated in Syria, but not before it had wrought incalculable damage to human life and culture in the region.

49. The Central American republic of Honduras is one of the most violent countries in the world; drug cartel activity and endemic official corruption feature prominently in citizens' lives, and more than a hundred environmental activists have been murdered there in recent years. Cáceres was raised among the native Lenca people, whose access to traditional (and ostensibly protected) territory was threatened by a planned network of hydroelectric dams along the Gualcarque River, a project spearheaded by a company called Desarrollos Energéticos S.A. The determined efforts of Cáceres (plus DESA's flagrant use of homicidal paramilitaries to achieve its aims) eventually caused

some nervous international investors to pull out, and she was honoured with the prestigious Goldman Environmental Prize. Still, the acclaim couldn't save her. The hitmen who carried out the assassination also left for dead her friend and houseguest, Gustavo Castro, who was shot in the face and hand. He later testified in court about her final, breathtakingly courageous moments.

50. The Elderhorsts were citizens of the Netherlands, where both passive and active (i.e. physician-assisted) forms of euthanasia were made legal in 2001. Cases of this kind are extremely rare–both members of a married couple hardly ever meet the legal criteria for state-sanctioned euthanasia at the same time–but in this instance, the request was deemed reasonable, and was presided over by medical professionals with family members in attendance.

BIBLIOGRAPHY

"Jockey Dies as He Wins His First Race; Hayes Collapses Passing the Winning Post." *New York Times*. June 5, 1923.

Alpern, Stanley B. *Amazons of Black Sparta: The Women Warriors of Dahomey*. London, 2011.

Ariès, Phillipe. *The Hour of Our Death: The Classic History of Western Attitudes Toward Death Over the Last One Thousand Years*. Trans. H. Weaver. London, 1981.

Bacon, John U. *The Great Halifax Explosion: A World War I Story of Treachery, Tragedy, and Extraordinary Heroism*. New York, 2017.

Barnard, Christiaan. *One Life*. London, 1970.

Beatty, Bill. *With Shame Remembered: Early Australia*. London, 1962.

Bever, Lindsey. "Elderly Couple Got 'Deepest Wish' — to Die Together — in Rare Euthanasia Case." *Washington Post*. August 17, 2017.

Blitzer, Jonathan. "The Death of Berta Cáceres." *New Yorker*. March 11, 2016.

Bradatan, Costica. *Dying for Ideas: The Dangerous Lives of the Philosophers*. London, 2015.

Brighton, Terry. *Hell Riders: The Truth About the Charge of the Light Brigade*. London, 2005.

Cartledge, Paul. *Spartans: An Epic History*. London, 2002.

Cowan, Ross. *For the Glory of Rome: A History of Warriors and Warfare*. Yorkshire, 2017.

Crespigny, Rafe de. *A Biographical Dictionary of Later Han to the Three Kingdoms (23 – 220 AD)*. Leiden, 2006.

Critchley, Simon. *Book of Dead Philosophers*. London, 2008.

Davidson, James W. *Samoa Mo Samoa: The Emergence of the Independent State of Western Samoa*. Melbourne, 1967.

Dockstader, Frederick J. *Great North American Indians: Profiles in Life and Leadership*. New York, 1977.

Drake, Benjamin. *Life of Tecumseh, and of His Brother the Prophet*. Cincinnati, 1841.

Galeano, Eduardo. *Mirrors: Stories of Almost Everyone*. Trans. M. Fried. New York, 2009.

Graff, Garrett M. *Only Plane in the Sky: The Oral History of 9/11*. New York, 2019.

Grynberg, Michal. *Words to Outlive Us: Eyewitness Accounts from the Warsaw Ghetto*. Trans. P. Boehm. London, 2004.

Hemming, John. *The Conquest of the Incas*. New York, 2012.

Hibbert, Christopher. *The French Revolution*. London, 1980.

Hibbert, Christopher. *The Road to Tyburn: The Story of Jack Sheppard and the Eighteenth-Century Underworld*. London, 2001.

Herodotus. *The Histories*. Trans. T. Holland. London, 2013.

Holland, Tom. *In the Shadow of the Sword: The Battle for Global Empire and the End of the Ancient World*. London, 2012.

Hoyland, Robert G. *In God's Path: The Arab Conquests and the Creation of an Islamic Empire*. Oxford, 2015.

Jackson, Peter. *The Delhi Sultanate: A Political and Military History*. Cambridge, 1999.

James, Clive. *The Book of My Enemy: Collected Verse 1958-2003*. London, 2003.

James, C. L. R. *The Black Jacobins: Toussaint L'Ouverture and the San Domingo Revolution*. London, 2001.

Jones, Peter. *Memento Mori: What the Romans Can Tell Us About Old Age and Death*. London, 2018.

Joseph, Eve. *In the Slender Margin: The Intimate Strangeness of Death and Dying*. New York, 2016.

Keith, Jeanette. *Fever Season: The Story of a Terrifying Epidemic and the People Who Saved a City*. New York, 2012.

Kellehear, Allan. *A Social History of Dying*. Cambridge, 2007.

Lakhani, Nina. "Who Killed Berta Cáceres? Behind the Brutal Murder of an Environment Crusader." *Guardian*. June 2, 2020.

Livy. *The War with Hannibal*. Trans. J. C. Yardley. London, 2011.

Matthews, Brander. *Molière: His Life and His Works*. London, 1910.

Montaigne, Michel de. *The Complete Essays*. Trans. M. A. Screech. London, 1993.

Moynihan, Colin. "Professor's Violent Death Came Where He Sought Peace." *New York Times*. April 19, 2007.

Murtagh, Peter. "Grim tale of slain Romeo and Juliet." Irish Times. July 25, 2008.

Nirvan, Kiran. *21 Kesaris: The Untold Story of the Battle of Saragarhi*. New Delhi, 2019.

O'Shea, Stephen. *Sea of Faith: Islam and Christianity in the Medieval Mediterranean World*. London, 2007.

Parker, Philip. *The Northmen's Fury: A History of the Viking World*. London, 2014.

Philbrick, Nathaniel. *In the Heart of the Sea: The Tragedy of the Whaleship Essex*. London, 2005.

Plato. *Last Days of Socrates*. Trans. H. Tredennick and H. Tarrant. London, 2003.

Price, John. *The Heroes of Postman's Park: Heroic Self-Sacrifice in Victorian London*. Stroud, 2015.

Procopius. *History of the Wars, Vol. 1, Books 1-2: The Persian War*. Trans. H. B. Dewing. Cambridge, 1914.

Rasmussen, Dennis C. *The Infidel and the Professor: David Hume, Adam Smith, and the Friendship That Shaped Modern Thought*. Princeton, 2017.

Schama, Simon. *The Story of the Jews: Finding the Words 1000 BCE–1492 CE*. London, 2013

Scott, Michael. *From Democrats to Kings: The Brutal Dawn of a New World from the Downfall of Athens to the Rise of Alexander the Great*. London, 2009.

Scott, Robert Falcon. *Journals*. Oxford, 2008.

Stewart, Jules. *Savage Border: The Story of the North-West Frontier*. Cheltenham, 2007.

Stewart, James B. *Heart of a Soldier: A Story of Love, Heroism. And September 11th*. New York, 2002.

Taitz, Emily et al. *The JPS Guide to Jewish Women: 600 BC –1900 CE*. Philadelphia, 2003.

Tacitus. *Annals and Histories*. Trans. A. J. Church and W. J. Brodribb. London, 2009.

Thompson, J. M. *English Witnesses of the French Revolution*. Oxford, 1938.

Tsunetomo, Yamamoto. *Hagakure: The Book of the Samurai*. Trans. W. S. Wilson. Boulder, 2012.

Turnbull, Stephen. *The Samurai*. Oxford, 2016.

Webb, Chris and Chocolatý, Michal. *The Treblinka Death Camp: History, Biographies, Remembrance*. Stuttgart, 2014.

Williamson, David G. *The Polish Underground 1939-1947*. South Yorkshire, 2012.

ABOUT THE AUTHOR

Matt Sturrock was born in 1974, and has worked for decades as a bookseller, editor, and freelancer in both Toronto and London, England. He has written for many publications, including the *National Post* and the *Globe & Mail*, and is a longtime contributor to the *Times Literary Supplement*. He currently resides in Vancouver, near the base of Mount Fromme. This is his first book.